Brief Humor:
Book of Law Cartoons

Featuring Cartoons From
Air Mail
Barron's
The New Yorker
and more!

Front Cover illustration: Danny Shanahan
Back Cover illustration: Leo Cullum
Introduction: Bob Mankoff
Editor: Darren Kornblut

Consider supporting https://familylegalcare.org

Cartoon Collections, LLC
10 Grand Central, 29th Floor
New York, NY 10017

For cartoon licensing information visit www.cartoonstock.com
Create a personalized version of this book at www.cartoonstockgifts.com

First edition published 2024

ISBN: 978-1-963079-17-3
Item # 49148

Introduction

As someone who has spent a considerable chunk of my life nestled between the inked lines of cartoons, where punchlines often hit closer to the mark than a well-aimed gavel, I'm thrilled to usher you into the world of legal cartoons.

This collection is more than just a series of drawings; it's a reflection of the legal profession's peculiarities, its idiosyncrasies, and, of course, its humor. The law, with its byzantine complexities and solemn rituals, might seem an unlikely source of comedy. Yet, it's in the arcane and often absurd that humor finds a fertile ground.

As you flip through these pages, you'll find that the world of legalities and litigations isn't just about statutes and precedents. It's also about human nature, the sometimes-comical dance of courtroom dramas, and the universal truths that emerge when justice wears a smile.

So, whether you're a seasoned attorney or simply a connoisseur of wit, I invite you to delve into these pages. So sit back, relax, and prepare to be entertained as our cartoonists take you on an humorous journey into the lighter side of the law.

Biz Monks

"*Well if I can't be a cowboy I'll be a lawyer for cowboys.*"

"It's clear from the replay that it was a leading question."

"Ladies and gentlemen of the jury duty..."

"Objection, Your Honor. Counsel is leading the witness."

"Trust me, you're going to be very happy you brought along legal representation."

"May I represent you across the street?"

"You're going to do time, but I'm trying to get it in dog years."

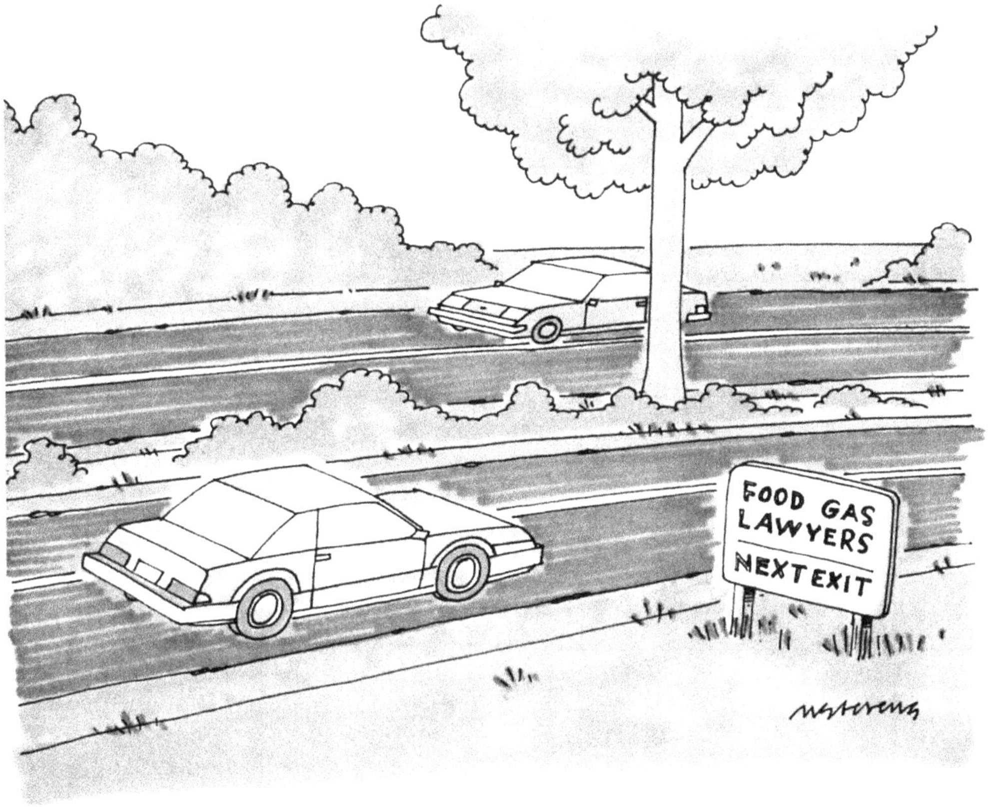
FOOD GAS
LAWYERS
NEXT EXIT

*"And this is my cousin Dave, who handles
the conventional wisdom."*

"You need to work on your pleading."

"My client demands that he be treated no better than any other celebrity."

CALL 1-800-JUSTICE FOR ALL YOUR LEGAL NEEDS

"Don't think of it as a conspiracy charge. Think of it as a buddy trial."

"Don't sign any binding agreements that we can't un–bind."

"YOU may see a great creation, Dr. Frankenstein...but I only see a great heck of a Product Liability Problem."

THE LAWYER OF OZ

Some of these bricks are a little loose.

We might want to fix that.

Also, the Wicked Witch's cousin is suing Oz for thirty billion dollars.

R.Chs

"The Court will allow the cape but will draw the
line at the wind machine."

"If you stop smoking now, you will add three years to your life. Since you are a lawyer, that's about six thousand billable hours."

"I'm afraid he left everything to charity... Oh, I see. I take it your name's Charity?"

"*And that's when he realized he wasn't on the partner track at all!*"

"I'll agree to a pre-nup if you'll agree to a non-compete clause."

"...for richer, for poorer, in sickness and in health,
until death or litigation do you part?"

"I can't answer that because of attorney-client fun duy."

"Yes, he cut paper, but rock hit him first
– that make my client a victim."

"*Three yummies, a pat on the head, and a 'Good doggy.'*
That's my client's final offer."

"Excuse me—this joke need a lawyer?"

"We're running late. Skip the brief,
just give me the tweet."

"I used to do it all myself, but now I have my lawyers handle it."

"Objection, Your Honor! The prosecution is combining dog years and people years in a callous and deliberate attempt to confuse the witness."

"I'd run it by legal myself, but they have a restraining order against me."

"*If you prick a corporation, does it not bleed? If you tickle it, does it not laugh? If you poison it, does it not die?*"

"*Will your client marry my client?*"

"*A pod of attorneys to see you, sir!*"

"We've decided that it will be better for his later development
if we speak to him only in legalese."

"I'd like to tell you what went on at work today,
but the legal department doesn't want us to do that anymore."

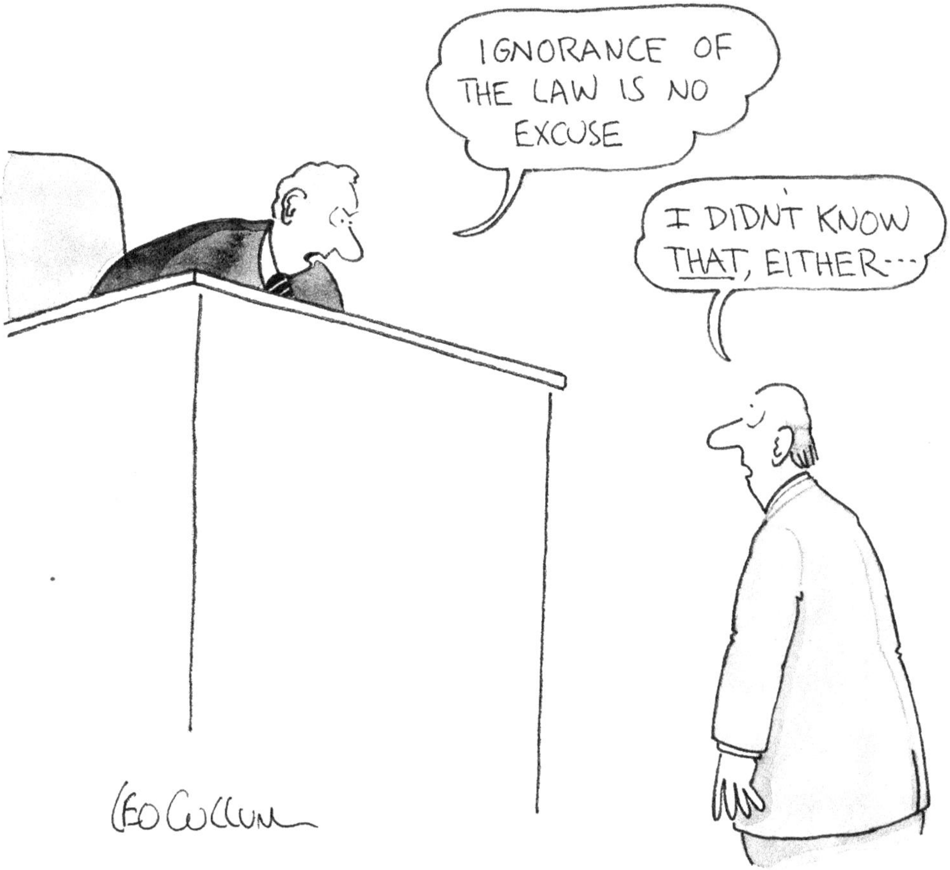
IGNORANCE OF THE LAW IS NO EXCUSE
I DIDN'T KNOW THAT, EITHER...
LEO CULLUM

"I'm not quite ready to order. My lawyers are still studying the menu."

"My client has nothing to leak at this time."

"We're fighting like—well, we're fighting."

"I do corporate, divorce, and malpractice, but
I'm most familiar with leash laws."

"You don't have to answer that."

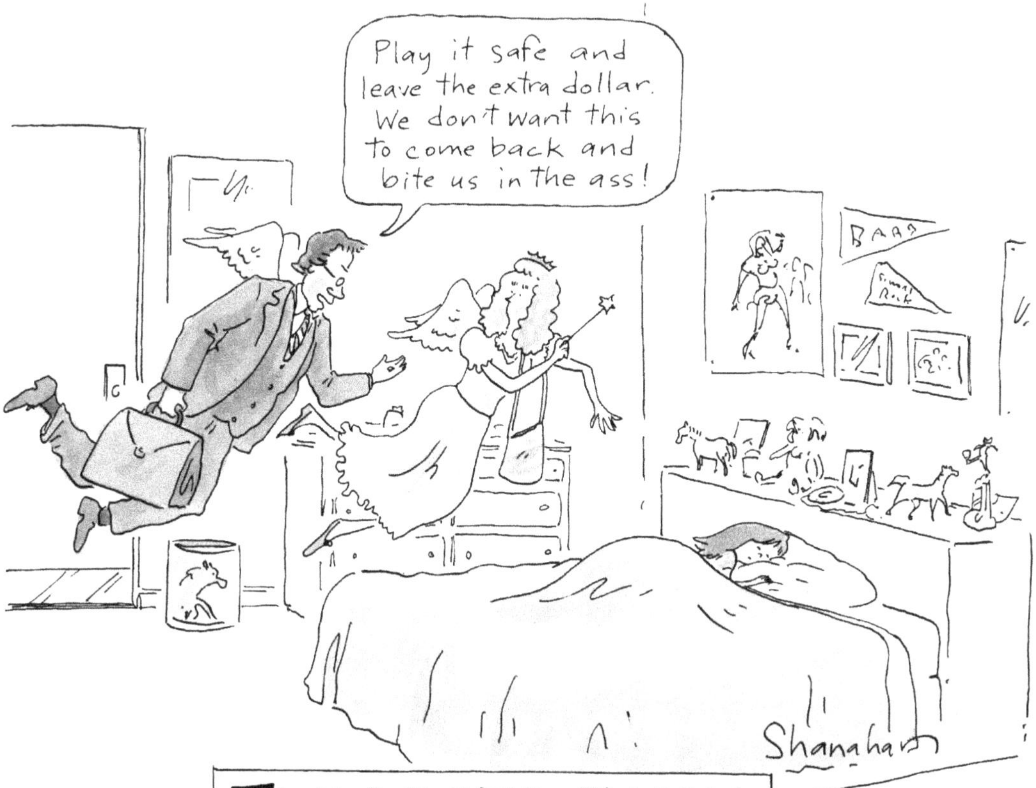
Play it safe and leave the extra dollar. We don't want this to come back and bite us in the ass!
Shanahan

THE LAWYER FAIRY

TOO MANY LAWYERS SPOIL THE BROTH

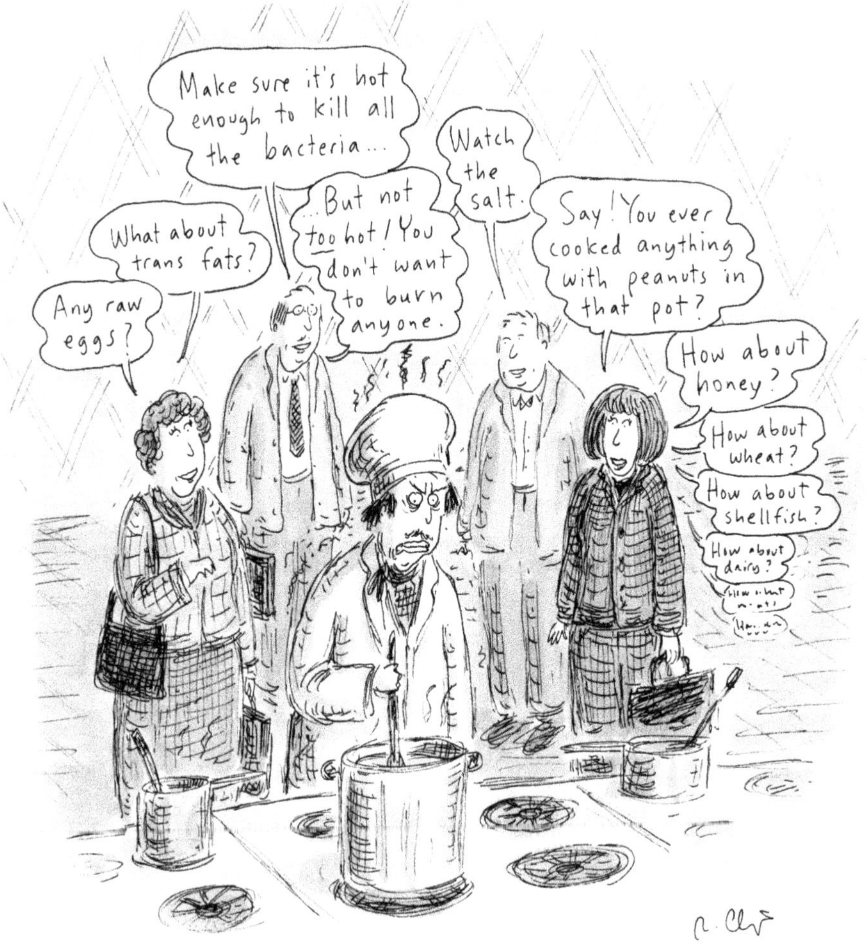
Any raw eggs?
What about trans fats?
Make sure it's hot enough to kill all the bacteria...
...But not too hot! You don't want to burn anyone.
Watch the salt.
Say! You ever cooked anything with peanuts in that pot?
How about honey?
How about wheat?
How about shellfish?
How about dairy?

"Who's up for archery waivers?"

"*And should you retain us, Mr. Hodal, you'll find that we're more than just a law firm.*"

DORIS K. ELSTON

BRAIN SURGEON · PROFESSIONAL
MODEL · ARTIST · LAWYER ·
plus
MOTHER OF FOUR

R Chast

"Do you have any picture books that could help
a child understand tort reform?"

So, worm, shall I tie you up in litigation?

Yes, please, and make it lengthy and expensive!

Shanahan

MISTRESS DOMINATRA, ESQ.

"The ones just out of law school are especially frolicsome."

"I may be a jackal-headed god of the underworld, Janet, but I'm also your lawyer."

MAZE
OF
LEGALITIES

DO NOT
ENTER
WITHOUT
AN
ATTORNEY.

Dave Carpenter

"What are you – some kind of justice freak?"

" 'Season's Greetings' looks O.K. to me. Let's run it
by the legal department."

"You can't plead cute."

"I see. And precisely what methods did you use to
determine that my client was a 'bad boy'?"

"Not guilty, Your Honor, and thank you for asking."

"Look, I'm not saying it's going to be today. But someday—someday—you guys will be happy that you've taken along a lawyer."

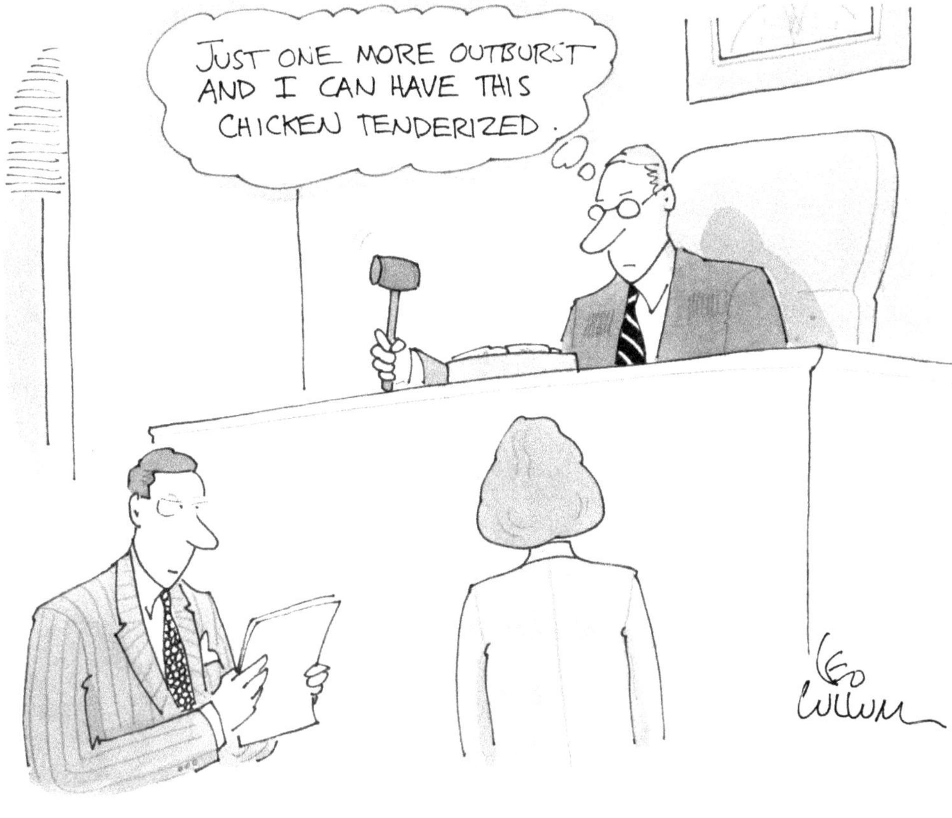
JUST ONE MORE OUTBURST AND I CAN HAVE THIS CHICKEN TENDERIZED.

"You got custody of us, mommy, because you're the very best attorney picker."

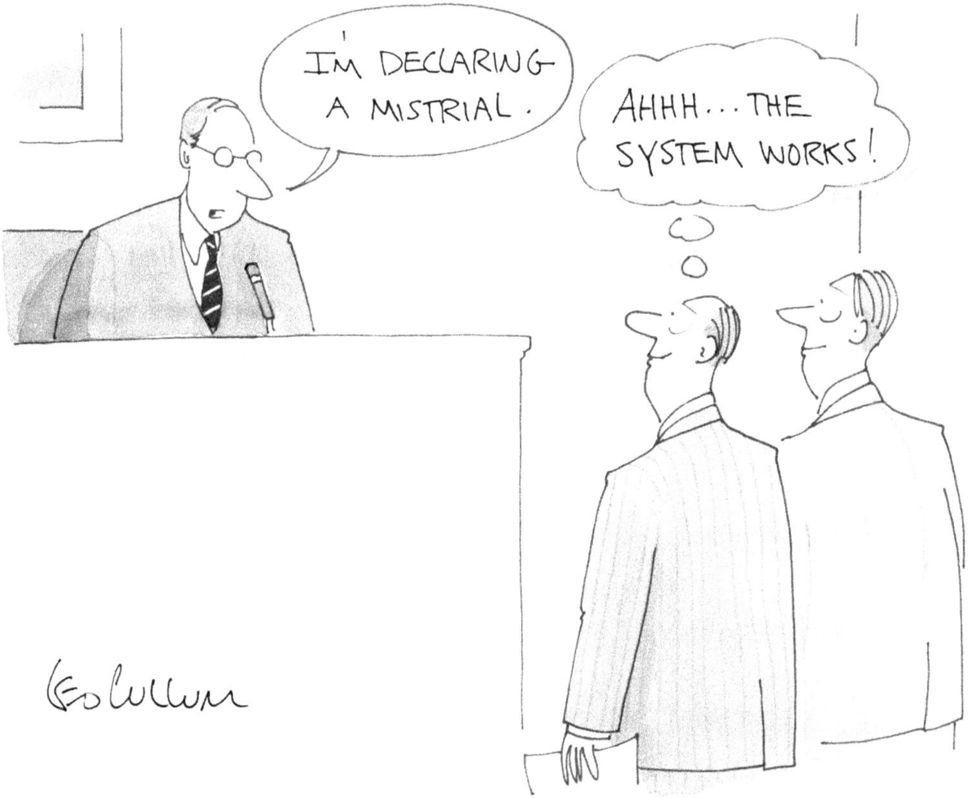
I'M DECLARING A MISTRIAL.
AHHH... THE SYSTEM WORKS!

"Well if that's _not_ the law it certainly _ought_ to be."

"Please go easy on my client, Your Honor.
He's already suffered enough with all the Twitter shaming."

"I prefer to err on the side of litigation."

"Your wish is my command... as long as it doesn't break the law
or harm children, animals, or the environment."

"Don't give me that. My lawyers assure me there's a
loophole in your menu's no-substitution clause big enough
to drive a truck through. Now, either I get my creamed
spinach instead of those fried onion rings or we'll continue this discussion in court."

"*I'm not talking to you as your lawyer – I'm talking to you as your best friend.*"

"As long as you don't sign anything in blood you should be O.K."

"Our religious friends are praying, our atheist friends are sending good thoughts, and our lawyer friends are figuring out who to sue."

"I'd like to avoid a costly and embarrassing trial but I could use the media exposure."

DUE DILIGENCE MAN

"*First I'm going to need everyone to sign these waivers.*"

"I've always said—juries are impossible to predict."

"I understand you're some fancy pants lawyer."

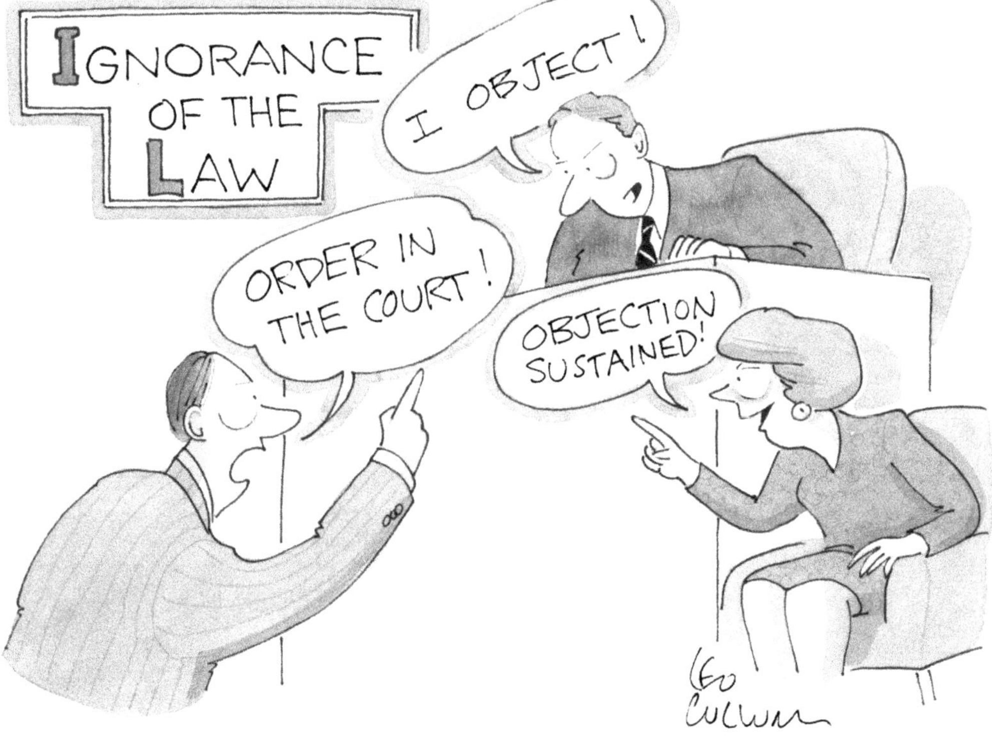
IGNORANCE OF THE LAW
I OBJECT!
ORDER IN THE COURT!
OBJECTION SUSTAINED!

"This marriage quiz was probably written by a divorce lawyer."

"We'll use the most expensive law firm. That way, if we lose, the board can't blame me for using a reasonable priced firm."

"*The road ahead is filled with danger.*
Take this lawyer for protection."

"You're absolutely sure my wife won't be able to find this?"

"*While this is by no means an admission of guilt we would like to settle out of court for 78 trillion dollars.*"

"*Does it ever cross your mind that we make a lot of money because no one else wants to do what we do?*"

"I lost it in a legal minefield."

"I'd like a sidebar, your honor."

"I'll have my people subpoena your people."

"And before you mail your valentines, please make sure your attorney reviews the sexual harassment waiver."

"It's a deal, but just to be on the safe side let's have our lawyers look at this handshake."

"There, there Mrs. Macklin—don't cry on billable time."

"Do you have a good attorney or a bad attorney?"

Index of Artists

www.ingramcontent.com/pod-product-compliance
Lightning Source LLC
Chambersburg PA
CBHW062333150426
42813CB00078B/2733